UTAH
JAZZ

UTAH
JAZZ

DAN ZADRA

CREATIVE EDUCATION

Photo Credit: Creative Education would like to thank NBA photographer Ron Koch (New York City) for the color photography in this series.

Published by Creative Education Inc., 123 South Broad Street, Mankato, Minnesota 56001.

ISBN: 0-88682-218-1

In 1825, an adventurous young trapper by the name of Jim Bridger made a discovery that turned him into a legend among his fellow mountain men. It seems that Jim and some pals were camped in Indian country along Utah's Bear River. They were curious about where the river might lead them.

"I'll find out!" exclaimed Jim, and he jumped in his buffalo boat and headed fearlessly down the river. Then he entered the rapids.

The tiny boat whirled through foaming water, crashing into rocks and bouncing off canyon walls. Jim hung on for his life. At last the river calmed down. After passing through an eerie marsh, Jim emerged on a tremendous body of water. He tasted it—and it was salty.

"It's the Pacific Ocean!" he exclaimed. But he was wrong. Jim Bridger had discovered Utah's Great Salt Lake, until then a secret known only to the Indians.

At first, city slickers in the East ignored Bridger's discovery. "Of what use is a 2,000-square-mile salt lake surrounded by desert?" they laughed.

Brigham Young and his Mormon followers had the answer. In 1847, they founded the religious community of Salt Lake City on the Jordan River, just a few miles from the lake itself. In time, the Mormon faithful developed irrigation techniques that transformed parts of the desert into rich and fertile land.

Today, Salt Lake City is a thriving metropolis, the capital city of Utah and the world headquarters of the Mormon Church. Since 1979, it has also been the home base for the subject of our story, the Utah Jazz of the National Basketball Association.

If Jim Bridger were alive today, chances are he'd be a loyal Jazz fan, for this is certainly his type of team. During its brief history in the NBA, Utah has shown itself to be an adventurous and impulsive club, one that has frequently drifted into troubled waters. Along the way, the team has endured tough times, snide remarks and occasional ridicule. But lately the laughter has subsided as the Jazz have slowly but surely moved their way up higher and higher on the NBA ladder, thanks in large part to Utah head coach Frank Layden.

One of the most humorous, outspoken and popular coaches in the league, Layden took the helm in December of 1981, shortly after the Jazz made their move to Salt Lake City. Prior to that, the club was headquartered in New Orleans, a city known as the jazz music capital of the world. That, of course, explains how the team originally got its nickname.

Our story begins in early 1974 with the announcement that a nine man group, headed by California entrepreneur Fred Rosenfeld, had agreed to pay $6.15-million for the right to establish the New Orleans Jazz as the 18th member of the NBA.

From the very beginning, Rosenfeld and his partners emphasized that the style of the new franchise would be in keeping with the style of New Orleans itself—bright, colorful, entertaining and outright jazzy. The team colors would be the boldest shades of purple, green and gold. The halftime spectacles at Jazz games would rival the pageantry and excitement of the city's famous Mardi Gras festivals. According to the owners, "Our fans will come to expect the unexpected. Game time will always be 'showtime' in New Orleans."

John Stockton, a deadly passer, dished out 670 assists in 1986-87, including a franchise record 22 in a game against the Lakers.

To prove they were serious, the Jazz went to Atlanta and completed a trade that made Mr. Showboat himself, Pete Maravich, their first player.

Better known as "The Pistol," Maravich came as close to being a one-man team as any player in NBA history. His fans pointed out that when Pistol Pete was "on," he could single-handedly dismantle even the toughest defenses with his tricky passing, fancy ball-handling and sonar shooting. Pete dribbled between his legs and passed behind his back while looking the other way. One of his trademarks was the long-range jumper, a shot he described as "comfortable for me at 40 feet on in."

But that's the problem with Pete, said his critics. He tries to do it all by himself. One man never has won nor ever will win an NBA championship by himself, Maravich included.

Of course, with a supporting cast like Maravich had that first season, the Jazz were no big threat to win a title of any type. Most of his teammates were players the other teams didn't want anymore. A New Orleans reporter referred to the Jazz lineup as a collection of "Division Too players, guys who are too old, too young, too injured, too troublesome or too quirky to hang on with a top NBA team."

Seven-foot center Neal Walk, for example, was a good all-around player, but his views were a little offbeat. New Orleans had high hopes for Walk until he dropped twenty pounds on a vegetarian diet. At mid-season the Jazz shipped him off to New York.

"The Pistol" goes up for a one-handed jumper. Pete Maravich came as close to being a one-man team as any player in NBA history.

The players shuffled in and out, and so did the coaches. Scotty Robertson was fired after the Jazz lost 14 of their first 15 games. His replacement, Butch van Breda Kolff, believed in fundamentals but pledged to deliver the action and excitement promised by the owners.

"I want everyone on my team to be sound and involved," said van Breda Kolff, "but I don't want a bunch of robots. There's a place in the game for flair, but it has to be at the right time."

With Maravich, every time seemed like the right time. Despite what the critics said, it was flashy, high-scoring Pete Maravich who kept the Jazz within striking distance night after night. He poured in 47 points to lead the Jazz to their very first road victory, 102-101 against the Atlanta Hawks. At home the fans followed his every move, flocking to two different arenas that year to see The Pistol strut his stuff.

And that's another story in itself. The owners' ambitious plans called for the Jazz to move to the comfy confines of the big Louisiana Superdome by year two. Meanwhile, however, the Jazz played the first part of their inaugural season at Municipal Auditorium, a cramped and dingy place in a rundown part of the city.

In December, they moved to rickety little Loyola Field House which wasn't much better.

Nate Williams

The Jazz grew attached to the place. "It's our snakepit," said Maravich.

Believe it or not, the court was elevated three feet above floor level, like a stage for a rock group. Restraining nets had to be strung around the sides of the court so the players wouldn't tumble down onto the spectators. The Jazz and their fans gradually grew attached to the place. "It's our snakepit," said Maravich.

The Jazz finished with a disappointing 23-59 record in 1974-75, but help was on the way. In the first round of the 1975 draft New Orleans snagged smooth-shooting Rich Kelley, a 7-foot center out of Stanford. Kelley's presence in the middle occupied enemy defenders and freed Maravich.

Rich Kelley

I can set up and shoot or get a decent pass off now, where before I was always double or triple-teamed," said Maravich who scored his 10,000th career point and made the NBA All-Star Team in 1975-76. The Jazz' record improved by 15 games to 38-44.

During the off-season, it was announced that veteran superstar Gail Goodrich of the Los Angeles Lakers would join the New Orleans backcourt in 1976-77. Jazz fans greeted the news with mixed emotions. Like Maravich, the 33-year-old Goodrich was a tremendous shooter, but skeptics predicted Pete and Gail would never be able to share the spotlight. Their egos would clash, and the team would be torn apart.

"That will never happen," said Maravich. "I don't care if it's Godzilla, I can play with anybody on a basketball court. With an intelligent, experienced player like Gail, there's no problem at all. He's a great shooter and I'm going to get the ball to him."

As it turned out, Goodrich played a steady back-up role during most of the year while Maravich soared to the

The new NBA scoring leader was Pete Maravich . . .

season of a lifetime. "The new NBA scoring leader was Pete Maravich, fully mature and every bit as spectacular at the age of 28 as had been predicted in his college days," wrote NBA historian Zander Hollander. "He averaged 31.1 points a game and had a 68-point game against the Knicks, a performance surpassed only by Wilt Chamberlain and Elgin Baylor in league history."

No room to roam: To stop Gail Goodrich (25), the Nets resort to double teaming.

Baylor himself had a front-row seat the night Pete had his 68-pointer against New York. You see, a few weeks earlier the Jazz had hired Baylor to replace coach van Breda Kolff. With Baylor calling the shots, the Jazz enjoyed an eight-game winning streak near the end of the season and finished with a 35-47 record.

Then a big, powerful truck came rolling into New Orleans just in time for the start of the 1977-78 season. Free agent Len "Truck" Robinson, a 6-foot-6, 240-pound power forward was a dream come true for Baylor and the Jazz. Described by Maravich as having "muscles on his muscles," Truck had a surprisingly sweet shot for a man his size and was a terror under the boards.

Robinson teamed up with centers Rich Kelley and Joe C. Meriweather and forwards Aaron James and Nate Williams. At last, the Jazz had a formidable frontline that could actually keep up with the club's talent-laden backcourt. The result was a season for the record books. Gail Goodrich topped the 17,000 career point mark. Robinson averaged 23 points per game and clinched the NBA rebound title with 1,288. Maravich and Robinson both made the East All-Star team. And the Jazz finished the season with 39 wins, the most ever, including a club record 10-game winning streak.

It should have been a time of joy and celebration, but there was trouble in the air. Although the Jazz had made great strides in 1977-78, they had still finished fifth in the Central Division, just a step above cellar-dweller Houston. Once again New Orleans had failed to make the playoffs, and the fans were growing restless.

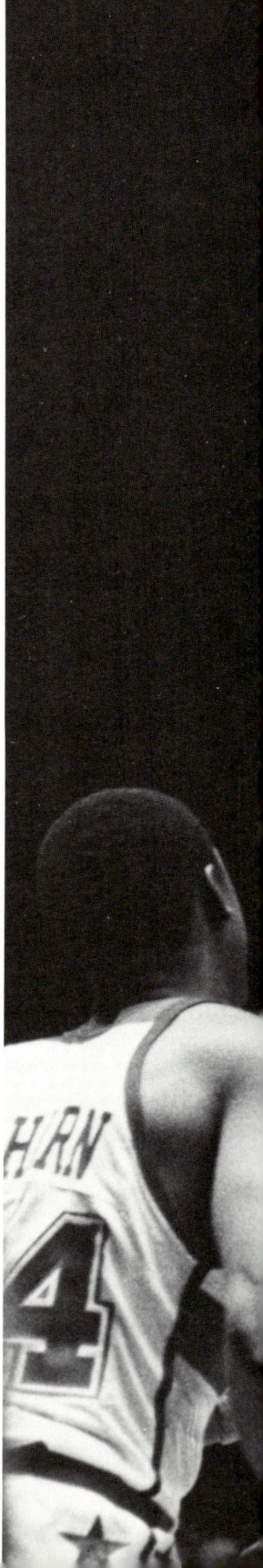

Surrounded by enemy Bullets, the great Adrian Dantley passes off in a game against the Bullets.

C

oach Baylor felt the pressure. There were times when he yearned to tear off his shirt and tie and join his players on the court. "I've never been in a situation like this before," said Baylor who had been the highest-scoring forward in the game for 12 seasons with the Lakers. Clearly, Baylor was accustomed to being a winning player, not a losing coach.

"The fans are entitled to have high expectations," he said, "but it takes time to build a top team. We're making headway. I would just ask that everyone be patient and supportive."

The fans were neither in 1978-79. When top scorers Robinson and Maravich were both sidelined with injuries, Baylor's hopes for a great season flew out the window. At mid-season, the Jazz had a mere 12 victories to their credit. In desperation, they traded Meriweather to New York for high-scoring forward Spencer Haywood. No help. When the club continued to struggle, the fans quit coming to the games. Attendance for the year dropped by approximately 30 percent. Slowly, sadly, the

season lurched to a disappointing close, and the door slammed shut on the era of the New Orleans Jazz.

In 1979, co-owners Sam Battistone and Larry Hatfield moved the Jazz from New Orleans to Salt Lake City. The folks in Utah were no strangers to the pro game. For several years the Utah Stars of the ABA had featured some of the top players and best action in that league. The Stars had folded in 1975, stranding several thousand fans who still yearned for big league basketball.

When the news hit that the Jazz were coming to Salt Lake City, the community rejoiced and immediately swung open the doors on the Jazz' new home court, the impressive 13,000-seat Salt Palace Center Arena. "Happy Days Are Here Again!" read the welcome banner, and indeed they were.

In the weeks leading up to the move, the Jazz had named Tom Nissalke to be their new head coach. Next, they had persuaded popular Frank Layden to be their new general manager. Everything moved swiftly from that point on.

On September 13, 1979, Layden engineered a trade with the Los Angeles Lakers that brought former Rookie of the Year Adrian Dantley to Utah in exchange for Spencer Haywood. It was Layden's opinion that the 6-foot-5, 210-pound Dantley was potentially "the best small power forward in the game."

When the news hit that the Jazz were coming to Salt Lake City, the community rejoiced . . .

On October 2, Layden traded Rich Kelley to New Jersey for Bernard King, John Gianelli and Jim Broyland, but the shake-up wasn't over yet.

On October 22, Pete Maravich scored 28 points to lead the Utah Jazz to their first regular season victory. It was to be one of The Pistol's final great performances in a Jazz uniform because within a month Adrian Dantley would rise up and become the team's new leader. In November, Dantley received his first NBA Player of the Week award and later led the West in scoring in the NBA All-Star Game. Dantley finished his spectacular season with a red-hot 28-point average. But Dantley's heroics came at Maravich's expense.

"The ironic thing is that Dantley is probably the guy most responsible for Pete's departure," said Layden after the Jazz waived Maravich on January 11, 1980. "If we didn't have Dantley, we'd need Pete's points and drawing power. Having Dantley made Pete expendable."

The Pistol was gone, but not forgotten. In tribute, the Jazz would retire his No. 7 jersey in 1985. In May of 1987, Pete Maravich would be inducted into the Naismith Memorial Basketball Hall of Fame shortly before his sudden and tragic death from a rare heart ailment.

As for the Jazz, they headed into the decade of the 1980s with their hopes resting squarely on the shoulders of Adrian Dantley. Layden, their outspoken general manager, had urged coach Nissalke to "get rid of all the losers. We'll just keep changing until we get guys who can win. Adrian is that kind of player. We want to build around him."

Superstar Adrian Dantley sparked the Jazz for seven seasons before being traded to Detroit for Kelly Tripucka and Kent Benson in 1987.

Darrell Griffith

To help out Dantley, Layden drafted Darrell Griffith in the first round of the 1980 draft. Griffith, a 6-foot-3 guard, was a brilliant dribbler and passer who, according to Layden, "could shoot from the shores of the Great Salt Lake and probably make it."

Together, Griffith and Dantley accounted for about half the points scored by Utah in 1980-81. Their stellar play helped ease the fans' disappointment over the club's 28-54 finish that season. Griffith became the unanimous choice for NBA Rookie of the Year. Dantley won the NBA scoring championship with a 30.7 average, including a whopping 50-pointer against his former team, the Lakers. "When I play against teams that have traded me, I kind of take it personally," grinned Dantley.

The following season, 1981-82, was pretty much a repeat of the year before. Once again, Griffith and Dantley churned out the points. Other than occasional bursts from rookie center Danny Schayes, however, the two Utah superstars received little help

Griffith could shoot from the shores of the Great Salt Lake . . .

from the rest of the Jazz. When the club finished the season with a record of 25-57, Nissalke was fired and general manager Frank Layden took over as head coach.

Now the fun began. Layden proved to be a good strategist, a great motivator and a definite crowd-pleaser. The Utah reporters loved the way he held court with them after the games, firing off colorful answers to their questions. He was funny, irreverent, brutally honest and highly quotable.

What are Utah's chances of winning the NBA Championship this year?" asked a reporter who was obviously trying to get Layden's goat at the start of the 1982-83 season.

"About the same as your chances of writing a Pulitzer Prize-winning story," laughed Layden, "but we'll try."

Layden began the year with a starting lineup that featured Dantley and Ben Poquette at forward, Danny Schayes at center, and Darrell Griffith and Rickey Green at the guards. Green, a flashy playmaker, proved to be a far better defensive player than anyone anticipated. And Schayes, though playing well, was gradually eclipsed at center by towering rookie Mark Eaton. At 7-foot-4, 290 pounds, Eaton already showed signs of becoming the league's top shot-blocker.

With a little luck, Layden might have guided the Jazz into the playoffs that season. Unfortunately, Dantley injured his wrist and missed the last 60 games. Even without their top scorer, however, Utah played far bet-

Adrian Dantley

ter than in years past and managed to improve their record to 30-52. It was a sign of good things to come.

The story of the Utah Jazz's 1983-84 season reads like a fairy tale come true. "The ugly duckling of the Midwest Division has become a beautiful swan," wrote a *Sporting News* analyst after the Jazz moved into first place on December 17 with a win over Golden State. Utah finished December with an 11-2 record, the best monthly record in Jazz history, and Layden was selected NBA Coach of the Month. From there, the story just got better and better.

On January 15, the Jazz moved to the top of the entire Western Conference and Layden earned the right to coach the West in the NBA All-Star Game, bringing Dantley and Green along with him. Layden told a Las Vegas reporter, "As far as I'm concerned, our entire starting lineup deserves to make the trip to the All-Star Game."

By season's end, four of the Jazz's starting five were NBA champs in at least one statistical category. Adrian Dantley averaged 30.6 points to lead the NBA in scoring. Rickey Green led in steals with 4.28 per game. Darrell Griffith was the leader in three-point accuracy. And big Mark Eaton was the league's top shot-blocker. Never before in the history of the league had a single team accumulated so many individual crowns in one season.

As far as I'm concerned, our entire starting lineup deserves to make the trip to the All-Star Game.

The Golden Griff: No. 35, Darrell Griffith was selected in the first round of the 1980 draft and became the 1980-81 NBA Rookie of the Year.

Utah won their first division title that year with an outstanding 45-37 record. They then advanced to their first-ever playoff series and easily defeated the Denver Nuggets in five games. By then, the entire state of Utah was abuzz with excitement. The prospect of Layden and the boys going all the way to the championship series seemed so real, so possible. But it was not to be. In the Western Conference semifinals, the sizzling Phoenix Suns finally rose up to defeat the Jazz in six games. Layden handled the pain of losing in the same way that he had been handling the joy of winning. . .with humor.

"Hey, don't worry about me, I've been practicing up on my losing," joked Layden, who had used a fad diet to lose 75 pounds during the course of the season. "I figure we're still America's team and I'm America's coach. People all over the world realize if the Jazz and their coach can make it, anybody can." Layden's achievements were so inspirational he was voted Coach of the Year and Executive of the Year by the NBA and *The*

Layden's achievements were so inspirational he was voted Coach of the Year . . .

Sporting News.

Respect. Secretly, every player yearns for it, but there's only one way to get it. Like a hug from a child, respect must be earned rather than demanded. A team or a player doesn't earn it overnight, they earn it over time. The Jazz, at long last, had broken the 40-win barrier, reaped an impressive crop of individual accolades, and seized a small place in the NBA spotlight.

Popular coach Frank Layden was crowned 1984 NBA Coach of the Year

But you can't be kidding yourself," said Dantley. "We know that one good season is pretty much meaningless. We want to string things out, get better, reach higher. People forget your name unless you can come back and do it again and again."

True Jazz fans will never forget the events that transpired over the next four seasons. The second half of the 1980s was a period of high achievement and continuous success that erased the loser image that had plagued the franchise during its first decade in the league. Players came and went, and there were problems along the way, but Layden's teams always found a way to battle their way into the playoffs by season's end.

A terrible start in 1984-85 was offset by a brilliant finish as the Jazz rebounded to post a 23-18 record during the second half of the season and defeat Houston in the first round of the playoffs. Eaton, who shattered the NBA shot-blocking record with 5.56 blocks per game, was named NBA Defensive Player of the Year, and the Jazz recorded their second consecutive 40-plus-win season, finishing at 41-41.

The mailman arrived for the 1985-86 season. Karl Malone, an extraordinary rookie forward out of Louisiana Tech, was called "The Mailman" because he always delivered. You want points? Rebounds? Blocked shots? Last second game-winners? Go to Malone. He'll come through time after time. The Jazz were glad they had him, too, because Darrell Griffith was sidelined with a foot injury for the entire season. Malone took up the slack, averaging 15 points per game, making the All-Rookie team, and sparking the Jazz to a 42-40 record and their third consecutive trip to the playoffs.

Mark Eaton, a rugged veteran out of UCLA, holds the Jazz career record for blocked shots.

But it was the following season that saw The Mailman really come into his own. In 1986-87, Malone set the league on fire, averaging 21.7 points and 10.4 rebounds. He was asked to do more mainly because Adrian Dantley was dealt to the Detroit Pistons for Kelly Tripucka and Kent Benson. Without Dantley, everyone had to contribute a little more. Eaton, Griffith and Green all did their part, as did third-year guard John Stockton. A great passer, Stockton dished out 670 assists, including a franchise record 22 in a game against the Lakers.

So even without Dantley, the Jazz clinched a playoff berth. In the first round, Utah bolted to a 2-0 advantage over Golden State, but somehow the Warriors rallied to take the next three games and the series. "We've got to work on our math," shrugged Layden who was disappointed but undaunted. "I reminded the guys that two wins and three losses adds up to no prize money."

Apparently, the Jazz learned their lesson. In 1987-88, the club rolled to a franchise best 47-35 record. Though the Portland Trail Blazers held the homecourt advantage in the first playoff round, Utah swiftly overpowered them, 3-1, and advanced to their biggest test ever, a showdown with the World Champion Los Angeles Lakers.

■ *Mark Eaton, seen here guarding Kareem Abdul Jabbar, was the 1984-85 NBA Defensive Player of the Year*

Los Angeles won easily in Game 1, but Utah bounced back to win the next two games as Malone scored 29 points in each.

The Lakers, feeling the pressure, won the next two games to go up 3-2 but the Jazz weren't through just yet. Brashly, Malone informed the press that there was just "no way" the Lakers could beat the Jazz again at the Salt Palace—and he was right. With The Mailman chalking up 27 points and Stockton adding 14 points and 17 assists, Utah humiliated the Lakers, 108-80, in Game 6 at Salt Lake City. Those who watched that nationally televised game would never again question whether the Utah Jazz were for real.

Though the Lakers won Game 7, 109-98, to take the series, Malone spoke for the entire Jazz team when he said: "Why should we hang our heads? We just took the best team in the world to seven games. They needed all

Those who watched . . . would never again question whether the Utah Jazz were for real.

they could muster to beat us. We're younger and hungrier, and I believe we have more firepower than they do. I think as time goes on, we will be the team to beat in the NBA."

Through the 1987-88 season Utah "6th Man" Thurl Bailey had accumulated nearly 300 games in which he scored in double figures.

With teammates such as John "Stock" Stockton and Thurl "Turbo T" Bailey at his side, Malone had good reason to be confident. Heading into the 1988-89 season, his sixth year in the league, Bailey had already accumulated nearly 300 games in which he had scored in double figures. Meanwhile, Stockton had rung up nearly 90 double-figure assists games.

"Statistics are fun to look at," said Layden, "but the important things about our team don't show up in the books. Players like Bailey and Stockton never miss a game, they never have an attitude problem, and they always put the good of the team ahead of themselves. It's teamwork with a capital T. That's what the Jazz are all about, and I'm proud to be a part of it."

■